THE WILD CATS

BY
JERLYN ANN NENTL

EDITED BY
DR. HOWARD SCHROEDER
Professor in Reading and Language Arts
Dept. of Elementary Education
Mankato State University

PRODUCED AND DESIGNED BY
BAKER STREET PRODUCTIONS
Mankato, MN

CRESTWOOD HOUSE
Mankato, Minnesota

CIP

LIBRARY OF CONGRESS CATALOGING IN PUBLICATION DATA

Nentl, Jerolyn Ann.
The wild cats.

(Wildlife, habits & habitat)
SUMMARY: Discusses the characteristics and habits of the wild cats of North America, including the lynx, bobcat, mountain lion, and others.
1. Felidae--Juvenile literature. 2. Mammals--North America--Juvenile literature. (1. Felidae. 2. Cats) I. Schroeder, Howard. II. Title. III. Series.
QL737.C23N46 1984 599.74'428 83-22506
ISBN 0-89686-249-6 (lib. bdg.)

International Standard Book Number:
Library Binding 0-89686-249-6

Library of Congress Catalog Card Number:
83-22506

ILLUSTRATION CREDITS:

Lynn Rogers: Cover
Phill and Loretta Hermann: 4, 43
Nadine Orabona: 7, 14, 23, 44
Bowhunting Productions: 8, 10, 31, 32, 33, 37, 38
Greg Yovan/Tom Stack and Associates: 13
Charles Summers/Tom Stack and Associates: 15
Alan G. Nelson/Tom Stack & Associates: 16, 19, 24-25
Jim Brandenburg/Photo Library: 20
Cheryl R. Todd: 28
Leonard Lee Rue III/Tom Stack & Associates: 41

CRESTWOOD HOUSE
Hwy. 66 South, Box 3427
Mankato, MN 56002-3427

TABLE OF CONTENTS

Introduction 5

Chapter I: Wild cats look and act alike 8
- Flech-eating predators
- Made for hunting
- The young are called cubs
- Playful — but fierce!

Chapter II: A wild range 14
- Short tails and tufted ears
- Solitary and nocturnal
- Preys on rabbits and deer
- Two ways of hunting
- Noisy mating

Chapter III: The mountain lion 29
- A long cat
- Lives in many habitats
- A feared cat
- A fantastic hunter
- Spotted cubs

Chapter IV: Jaguar, ocelot, jaguarundi, margay . 42

Chapter V: 45

Map: 46

Index/Glossary: 47

An African lion, one of the largest members of the cat family.

INTRODUCTION:

"ROA-OA-OA-AR-AR-ARGH!"

The sound echoed throughout the zoo, as John and Caroline walked through the gates.

"I love those big cats," Caroline said, turning in the direction of the roar. "Let's go look at them first."

"I don't like to look at animals in the zoo," John protested. "I'd much rather see them in the wild."

"Well, you won't hear that kind of a roar in the wild," Caroline told him. "Not in North America anyway. We don't have any of those big cats here."

"Are you sure?" John asked her. "I thought all wild cats roared."

"So did I, until I started studying them," Caroline said. "But they don't. Only the really big ones, like the lion and tiger, can roar. I don't think I'll ever be able to see them in the wild, so I'd like to see them here."

CHAPTER ONE:

Wild cats look and act alike

There are no wild lions or tigers in North America. These huge, roaring cats live in the wild on other continents. The wild cats native to North America are smaller. This book will focus on the three most common wild cats: the bobcat, lynx, and mountain lion. Chapter Four will also take a brief look at four other cats that are found mainly in countries south of the United States: the jaguar, ocelot, jaguarundi, and margay. All of these wild cats yowl, scream, meow and purr, but they do not roar. They cannot roar. The reason they cannot roar is because they are missing the small bones at the base of their tongues that make roaring possible.

Yet all wild cats, big or small, are very much alike. Except for their size and the color of their coats, they all look very much alike. Except for the sounds they make, they all act very much alike, too.

First, we will take a look at the things that apply to all of the North American wild cats.

Except for the jaguar, the mountain lion is the largest wild cat in North America.

Flesh-eating predators

Wild cats all belong to the same large group, or order, of animals that scientists call *Carnivores.* These are the animals that eat flesh. They are predators, which means they hunt and kill other animals for their food. North American wild cats may eat animals as big as a moose or as small as a mouse. They may also eat birds, fish, and sometimes, reptiles. What they eat depends on the types of animals that live in their area. Wild cats may lie in wait and spring upon their victim. Or they may stalk their victim, following its every step until the moment for the kill is right. Few animals prey upon the cats. If pursued, wild cats will usually try to get away. If there are trees in the area, the cats will climb into them and hide.

All wild cats like to hide in trees.

The wild cats of North America often sleep through the long daytime hours safely sprawled out on a tree branch or rocky ledge. They will also bed down in hollow logs or curl up on the ground among plants or brush. In bad weather, they take shelter beneath rocky ledges, under rock or brush piles, and in caves, cracks, and crevices.

The cats do not hibernate or have a dormant period during the winter. They are active all year.

Wild cats are trim, but very muscular animals. They have heads that look quite round. Their whiskers are long, and their jaws are strong. Wild cats have sharp teeth meant for cutting through the flesh of animals that they catch. The cats do not grind or crush their food. They bite off a chunk and swallow it whole.

A cat's tongue is covered with sharp, pointed bumps called *papillae*. These sharp points are slanted backwards. They are used by the cat to lick the last bit of flesh off the bones of animals it kills. The *papillae* also help clean the cat's coat as the cat licks its fur.

Made for hunting

If wild cats are not bothered by people, they are active both day and night. Their large, round eyes are especially equipped for this kind of life. The

A cat's eyes are very sensitive to light. This mountain lion can see well in both daylight and the dark.

pupils of a cat's eyes are very sensitive to light. They expand greatly in the dark to let in as much light as possible. In the daylight, they contract to narrow slits. This keeps out as much sunlight as possible. These slits are vertical, which means they extend from top to bottom rather than from side to side. The cat is the only animal to have such vertical eye slits. The wild cats that live near people are nocturnal. This means they are most active at night. They usually sleep during the day to avoid people.

Unlike some animals, wild cats have very keen eyesight. They also have a sharp sense of smell. Their hearing is excellent, too. These traits make them excellent hunters.

All cats are digitigrade. Digitigrade animals walk on their digits, or toes, rather than the soles of their feet. The back part of their foot is raised. The cats have thick pads on the bottom of their feet. These pads help them to prowl silently through the countryside. A wild cat's usual gait is a walk or trot. When running at high speed in a chase, however, they bound along the ground in great leaps.

Wild cats have four toes on each hind foot and five toes on each forefoot. However, only four of the toes on the forefoot touch the ground. The fifth toe is small and is located on the part of the foot that is raised.

Each toe has a long, sharp, curved claw. The claws are retractile, which means they can be pulled back in. This helps keep them from wearing down and becoming blunt. A wild cat uses its claws to catch and hold its prey. It also uses them to climb up trees. They keep their claws sharp and clean by scratching them on trees.

The young are called cubs

It is the female's job to raise the young, usually called cubs. The young of the smallest wild cats are sometimes called kittens. They are all altricial, which means they are quite helpless at birth. When they are born, they can't open their eyes and there are no openings in their ears. They are covered with soft fur. The mother cat nurses her young for two or three months. Later, she brings fresh meat to them. When the cubs are bigger and strong enough to follow her, they learn to hunt.

Playful — but fierce!

Wild cats often act like overgrown house cats. They can be very playful, especially during the mating season. The big cat, in the wild, often washes its face with its front paws just like the small house cat. Wild cats have a mild, pleasant look on their faces most of the time. Yet they can look very fierce, especially when defending themselves or their cubs. They often bare their teeth in a snarl. Their eyes blaze like fire!

Even a bobcat can look fierce when it snarls!

Wild cats are shy animals. Most of them avoid humans if at all possible. This makes them very hard to see in the wild. Most people will only see wild cats in a zoo.

Now that you know some things about wild cats in general, it's time to take a closer look at each of the most common types — the lynx, bobcat, and mountain lion.

CHAPTER TWO:

A wide range

The most common wild cats on the North American continent are the lynx and the bobcat. Because they look and act very much alike, they will be discussed at the same time.

The lynx lives in the North, from the Arctic Circle to the northern United States. Its scientific name is *Felis lynx.* The bobcat lives father south, from southern Canada to Mexico. Its scientific name is *Felis rufus.* The ranges of the lynx and bobcat overlap along the Canada-United States border.

To be more exact, the lynx lives across Canada from Newfoundland, Labrador, and Quebec in the east to British Columbia and the Yukon in the west.

The lynx (left) is more gray in color than the bobcat (right).

In Alaska it lives throughout the mainland except for the Panhandle and the Seward Peninsula. The lynx can be found in the lower forty-eight states around the Great Lakes, and in the Adirondack Mountains of New York. It also lives throughout the Pacific Northwest and along the Rocky Mountains as far south as Utah.

The bobcat is found in all the lower forty-eight states of the United States. However, it is not very common in the Plains states. It also lives throughout northern Mexico and the southern edge of Canada.

In general, the lynx lives where the cold, north wind blows. The bobcat likes warmer places.

The lynx favors forests of pine and fir trees for its habitat. At times, it can also be found in swampy muskeg bogs or on the tundra of the Far North. The bobcat is found in a much wider variety of habitat. It lives in forests and swampy areas like the lynx. Yet it also lives on open grasslands, in rocky canyons, and in deserts.

Short tails and tufted ears

Both cats have short, stout bodies, with long, muscular legs. Their hind legs are slightly longer than their forelegs. This gives them a rather strange appearance. Their back arches upward toward the base of their tail. Their rump is slightly higher than their front shoulders.

The lynx has much bigger, furrier feet than the bobcat. Its feet are like snowshoes, helping the lynx

The lynx has large feet to help it move over snow.

move swiftly over the snow. Its longer fur also helps insulate the lynx against the cold of the north country. The bobcat's feet are smaller and not so well-furred. It does not live in country that is as cold and snowy. Its fur is slightly shorter, too.

The male lynx measures about three feet (90 cm) long. Its tail is usually no more than four inches (10 cm) long. It stands about two feet (60 cm) tall at the shoulder and weighs twenty to thirty pounds (9.1-13.6 kg). The heaviest weight reported for a male lynx is forty pounds (18 kg).

The male bobcat is about two-and-a-half feet (75 cm) long. It has a six or seven inch (15-18 cm) tail. The male stands about fifteen inches (38 cm) tall at the shoulders and weighs fifteen to twenty pounds (7-9 kg).

The female cats of both types are slightly smaller in size and weigh less than the males. Because of their thick coat of soft, fluffy fur, both cats look larger than they really are.

The lynx is light gray streaked with brown. Its throat, belly, and the inside of its legs are a grayish-white with brown streaks. Its tail has a black tip. Its small, pointed ears are gray. At the tip of each ear there is a pointed tuft of black hair. This tuft is sometimes as long as one inch (2.5 cm). On each cheek is a "ruff" of long hair that is marked with a black stripe.

The bobcat's coat is yellowish-brown or reddish-brown, with dark brown or black markings. Its underparts are a yellowish-gray, with brown or black marks. Unlike the lynx, it has spots on its belly. The tip of its tail is black only on the topside. The bobcat's ear tufts and cheek ruffs are much shorter than those of the lynx. Some bobcats don't have any tufts.

Both cats molt, or shed, their body fur. The time of molting varies, according to the climate in the region where each cat lives. Those in warmer climates shed their fur earlier than those in colder climates.

The bobcat molts twice a year. In the spring, it sheds its heavy winter coat. It is replaced with a thinner, lighter coat for the summer. In the fall, this light-weight coat is replaced with a new, thicker coat of fur for the winter. Bobcats in warmer, drier areas will have a shorter, thinner coat of fur, even in the winter months. This helps them stay cooler. Their coats will often be lighter in color, too. This helps them blend with their desert environment.

The lynx molts only once a year. It sheds its heavy winter coat in the spring. A new winter coat grows again throughout the summer months.

Like many other cats, the lynx and bobcat are valued for their soft fur. Because of this, they are hunted and trapped. Their pelts are sold on the fur trading market.

Solitary and nocturnal

Adult lynxes and bobcats are solitary animals. This means they live alone. Most of the time they are nocturnal, or active at night. If they are not living near people, they will also be active during the day.

Each cat lives within a territory called a home range. A home range may be less than a mile square (2.6 sq km), or as large as seventy-five square miles (195 sq km). The size varies with the terrain of the

A bobcat drinks from a stream.

land and the amount of prey available. If food is scarce, a cat will enlarge its home range. The size of a home range also varies with the sex of the cat and the season of the year. Male lynxes and bobcats have larger home ranges than female cats.

Within each home range is a den site. Usually it is a favorite rocky ledge. This place is used for resting and sleeping. During the mating season, it is a meeting center. The rest of the year, the resident cat will defend its special place against any intruder. Most of the time, other adult cats simply stay away from these private places. That way they avoid a fight.

The lynx enjoys a private place.

Preys on rabbits and deer

The main prey of the lynx is the snowshoe hare. When these white, fluffy rabbits are abundant, the lynx does well. If hares are scarce, the lynx goes hungry. In lean times, lynxes roam far beyond their home range looking for snowshoe hares. If they cannot find any, they will turn to other small mammals and birds for food. At these times, they eat mice, squirrels, chipmunks, grouse, and partridges. They may also kill foxes, deer, antelope, and mountain sheep.

The lynx rarely, if ever, preys on livestock. A few attacks on poultry and sheep have been reported. As a rule, this happens when the livestock is left untended. Unless it is starving, a lynx seldom enters a farmyard.

The bobcat has a much wider variety of prey than the lynx. It eats almost any mammal, bird, or reptile. Its prey may be as small as mice or as large as deer. The bobcat prefers the cottontail rabbit. If food is scarce in the wild, bobcats will raid farms and ranches. They eat poultry such as chickens, ducks, geese, or turkeys. They also will eat lambs and piglets.

Both cats prefer fresh meat, as long as prey is available. The bobcat regularly caches, or stores, leftover meat for a later meal. It uses its forepaws to scrape leaves, grass, twigs, or snow over the carcass. The lynx may partly cover carcasses of smaller animals. Most of its leftover meat, however, is simply left behind.

Bobcats do not face food shortages as often as the lynx. They regularly hunt a wider variety of prey, and cache what they do not eat for a later time.

Scientists are not sure exactly how the lynx or bobcat kills its prey. They know that both cats are able to bite very rapidly. Their teeth can puncture a victim many times in only a few seconds. Most often, these cats bite their victims in the throat. The victim either bleeds to death or dies of strangulation. These cats may also bite their victims at the base of the skull. This probably cuts the spinal cord.

Two ways of hunting

The bobcats and lynxes have two ways of hunting. They may stalk their prey. This means they creep in as close as possible before making a dash to capture it. Or they may lie in wait until a victim passes by their hiding place. Then they attack with a quick leap.

These hiding places are often called "hunting beds." They are lookouts. Often they are in areas where prey is most abundant and active. The cat crouches down and waits, slowly moving around in a circle. After awhile, the cat has packed down a round area, or bed, in the grass, plants, dirt, or snow. Its front paw prints may show along the outside edge of the circle.

The wild cats sometime miss their prey when they pounce. If the prey runs, they may chase it. Neither cat is a very good runner over long distances. They tire easily. However, they may silently walk for many miles when looking for prey, never getting tired.

In spite of their small size, the lynx and bobcat can be fierce fighters. Their strength is well-known. They

Both the lynx and the bobcat (pictured) are fierce fighters.

A bobcat takes a look at its territory from a fence post.

can be very brave, sometimes attacking animals many times larger than they are. If cornered, they have even attacked people. Attacks on people, however, are very, very rare.

These wild cats are sometimes wasteful animals. At times they keep on killing even though their hunger has been satisfied. Scientists believe that the instinct to hunt may be as strong, if not stronger, than their need to eat.

Noisy mating

Lynxes and bobcats mate in late winter. The exact month depends upon the climate in the region where they live. Those in the warmer climate usually mate earlier in the year than those in the colder climates. Bobcats living in the South, where it is warm all year, may even mate a second time. The lynx only mates once a year. Both cats are several years old before they mate for the first time.

A lynx or bobcat may leave its home range to pursue a mate. Each one seeks a mate of its own kind. Several males may court one female. They playfully run beside her, bumping into her. If the weaker males do not finally step aside, the strongest male will fight them off. Then he will mate with the female. He may chew on her neck before and after mating, just like house cats do. She may meow and yowl loudly. He often answers with a deep growl or purr. The two may hunt and feed together for a short time. However, the bond between them does not last long. The male soon goes his own way, leaving the female to await the birth of the kittens.

The kittens are born after an eight or nine week gestation period. This period is the developing time before birth when the female carries her young inside her body. Most litters are born in the spring, from April to June. If a bobcat has a second litter, it is born in the fall.

Lynx and bobcat kittens may be born in a hollow log, a dense thicket, a clump of timber beneath a rocky ledge, or in a pile of rocks. There are usually two to four kittens in a litter. A lynx kitten is grayish-buff in color. It has dark brown or black streaks on its back, sides, and the outside of its legs. A bobcat kitten is yellowish-brown, with faint marks on its back and sides, and dark streaks on its face. The streaks on its face fade as the bobcat kitten gets older. The marks on its back and sides become darker.

The mother cat protects her kittens fiercely, but sometimes she is not successful. Because the kittens are so small and helpless, they may be killed by other predators, such as foxes or owls. Adult male cats may also kill young of their own kind.

The kittens go out hunting with their mother after they are a few months old. Then they are strong enough to follow along behind her or playfully run ahead. Such play is important. By chasing and pouncing on each other, they learn how to hunt for their food. By playfully fighting each other, they learn how to fight other animals.

The kittens stay with their mother until fall. During this time they learn how to take care of themselves. In the colder north country, kittens may stay with their mother until the spring. Living with her helps them stay warm through the cold winter months. Once the kittens have left their mother, however, they may roam for several years before they find a home range that they can call their own. Older adult cats do not seem to mind the presence of these younger cats on their home ranges. Most of the time they simply stay away from each other.

The lynx and the bobcat may live ten to twelve years in the wild. In captivity, they have been known to live twenty years or longer.

This bobcat has no ear tufts.

CHAPTER THREE:

The mountain lion

Another, bigger wild cat also lives in North America. It is the mountain lion. Except for the jaguar, it is the largest of all North American wild cats. It is the fifth largest cat in the world. Experts think that the mountain lion is the best hunter of all the wild cats.

At one time, this cat had one of the largest ranges of any land mammal in history. It was found across all of North and South America — from the Arctic Circle in the North to the Strait of Magellan in the South.

Today, its range still extends from the Canadian Yukon in the North to the southern Tip of Argentina in South America. However, it is now extinct in most of the northern parts of its range. In the United States most mountain lions are now found only in the western states. In Canada, only Alberta and British Columbia have a fair number of mountain lions. Small populations also live in the states along the Gulf of Mexico. The mountain lion still exists in large numbers in Mexico and countries to the south.

There are two main reasons that mountain lions

no longer exist in most areas of the North where it once did — people and deer. Years ago it was common for people to kill any mountain lion they saw, since the cats preyed on livestock. People were also afraid of these large wild cats. As land was settled, the mountain lion often lost the habitat it needed to survive.

An even bigger problem, however, was the disappearance of the mountain lion's favorite food, the deer. During the late 1800's and early 1900's, deer herds were badly thinned out in most parts of the eastern United States and southern Canada. Without the food it needed, the mountain lion could not survive. Modern game management has once again built-up deer herds, and an interesting thing is happening. There are reports of mountain lions in areas where they haven't been seen for many, many years!

It is not surprising that a cat that lives in so many places has many different names. Mountain lion or cougar are the names used in the western United States and Canada. People in the states surrounding the Gulf of Mexico call it the panther. Those in South America and Mexico call it the puma. The pioneers often called it the catamount, or "cat of the mountain."

Scientists have named it *Felis concolor.*

This old male cougar was photographed in the mountains of the western United States.

A long cat

The mountain lion is a long cat with a long, heavy tail. It has a small, round head. Its legs are short, but very strong. The mountain lion has very powerful shoulders. Its rather large ears have no tufts of hair at the tips. It has no cheek ruffs like the lynx or bobcat, either. The mountain lion has yellow eyes and long whiskers.

The size of the mountain lion varies. Adult males

An adult male mountain lion can weigh two hundred pounds (91 Kg).

may be four to eight feet (1.2-2.4 m) in total length, and weigh from one hundred forty to two hundred pounds (65-91 kg). They stand twenty-seven to thirty inches (68-76 cm) at the shoulders. Females are usually a little smaller than the males. The largest mountain lion ever reported weighed two hundred and sixty pounds (118 kg). It was nine-and-a-half feet (3 m) long!

A mountain lion is tawny brown in color over most of its body. Its chin, throat, breast, belly, and

A mountain lion is creamy white on its chin, throat, and belly.

the insides of its legs are a creamy white. The backs of its ears and the sides of its muzzle are dark brown. It has no markings at all on its body. There is a little tuft of hair at the tip of its tail, however. This tuft is dark brown or black.

The mountain lion's fur is thick and lies close to its body. The thickness changes according to the season of the year and the climate where the mountain lion lives. Those living where it is colder will have slightly thicker coats. A thicker fur coat helps keep them warm. All mountain lions molt, or shed, some of their fur during the summer when the weather is warm.

A mountain lion is a plain looking cat. Its fur has no value on the fur-trading market. Its skins, however, are sometimes sold as rugs.

Lives in many habitats

The mountain lion can live in many types of habitat. This includes forests of all kinds. It lives in evergreen, deciduous and tropical rain forests. It also lives in grasslands, swamps, and deserts. It can be found in thickets, rocky ridges, canyons, and ravines.

Each mountain lion has its own home range. The size of these home ranges varies. As a rule, a male mountain lion, living in an area where food is scarce, will have the largest home range. Females have smaller home ranges than males. Most mountain lions will hunt over an area that is between one hundred and one hundred fifty square miles (259-388 sq km).

A mountain lion often has a small favorite place where it sleeps and rests. It prefers an elevated spot or ledge so it can watch the area around it. The rest of its home range is a hunting area. The mountain lion is a solitary cat. It lives alone. Mountain lions will sometimes defend their home ranges, but most of the time, they just avoid each other. The hunting areas of males and females may even overlap.

A feared cat

As a rule, the mountain lion is harmless — unless it is cornered or is a female defending its cubs. This big cat does have the unusual habit of watching and stalking people. It is powerful enough to kill an unarmed person at any time. Attacks on humans, however, are very rare. These big cats seem to watch and stalk people because they are curious about them. In fact, deer have been seen doing the same thing. However, this habit of stalking people is one of the reasons mountain lions were killed years ago.

Another reason people fear the mountain lion is

the loud, long scream some people say they have heard it make. They describe it as a blood-curdling cry that sounds like the cry of a very frightened person or a train whistle. Other people, however, who have lived near mountain lions, say they have never once heard such a scream. At this time, no one knows why some mountain lions seem to "scream" and some do not.

A fantastic hunter

The mountain lion is a very graceful cat. It moves at a swift, smooth trot. This cat is known for its great strength and speed. It can bound across the ground covering twenty feet (6 m) at a time. A leap of forty feet (12 m) has been reported.

Like other wild cats the mountain lion is a predator. It preys on whatever it can find. Its favorite prey, though, is deer. It may also kill mammals as small as mice, rabbits, and skunks, or as large as elk and moose. In Florida, it also preys on raccoons, wild hogs, and armadillos. The mountain lion hunts both day and night. If bothered by people, the mountain lion will be more active at night.

Mountain lions seem to hunt in a circle around their home range, zigzaging back and forth. They leave some areas alone for days and often weeks at a time. If food is scarce, a mountain lion may travel thirty to fifty miles (48-80 km) on a hunting trip. It usually does not kill more than one deer, or an equal amount of small game per week.

The mountain lion stalks its prey in complete silence. Sometimes it may lie in wait for it, crouching low to the ground. Its long tail nervously twitches back and forth. When its prey is within range, it will rush out and jump upon it. Smaller prey are most often killed instantly, with a bite to the throat. The

A mountain lion can kill very quickly.

mountain lion attacks larger prey by leaping onto its back. It grasps the victim at the neck and shoulders with the claws on its front paws. It digs the claws on its hind paws into the victim's sides. Then it quickly breaks the spinal cord with a bite to the base of the skull. The kill is usually finished in a flash. This amazing ability to stalk within leaping distance is why it's so hard for people to get a look at a mountain lion. This cat is a master at staying hidden!

A mountain lion may feed on its kill right on the spot, or it may drag the carcass to a more hidden

The mountain lion is a very good stalker.

area. It has been known to move carcasses heavier than itself! A mountain lion usually caches, or stores, what it does not eat. Using its forepaws, the mountain lion covers the carcass with brush, sticks, and leaves. It may return two or three times to feed on its kill.

A mountain lion may sometimes kill livestock, like sheep, goats, cattle, or horses. This seems to happen when wild prey is scarce. Mountain lions sometimes kill more livestock than they need to eat. Livestock is usually found in groups and is easy to kill in large numbers. For example, a mountain lion may find a flock of sheep and kill ten or more in one night. Yet it may eat only one of them — or none at all!

This habit of killing livestock has brought the mountain lion into serious conflict with people. The killer cat is often hunted with a pack of dogs. Once the dogs have treed the cat, it is shot. Some ranchers and farmers would prefer to see all the mountain lions in their area killed. In certain areas a bounty is paid to those who kill mountain lions.

Spotted cubs

Mountain lions may breed at any time during the year, but they only mate every two or three years. Like the lynx and bobcat, several males may court a single female. There may be violent fights among the males. The strongest one mates with the female. The mates may stay together for several weeks, hunting and resting. Then once again the cats go off on their own. Scientists think the same cats may mate again in two or three years if their home ranges are close together.

After a gestation period of about ninety days, the female is ready to give birth. She beds down in a den among rocks, brush, or plants. It is a simple den, with just enough cover to keep out the sun and the rain. Her litter may have one to six cubs. Usually there are two or three.

Mountain lion cubs are a light brown like the adults. Their backs are sprinkled with spots of black or dark brown. These spots help camouflage, or hide, them from predators. The spots are very clear until a cub is three or four months old. Then they gradually fade.

Mountain lion cubs nurse until they are two or three months old. Then they begin to hunt with their mother. Like the lynx and bobcat mothers, she protects her young fiercely. Because a male mountain lion will sometimes kill a cub, the female is very aggressive toward any male that comes too close. The cubs remain with the female for about two years. At that time, she is ready to mate again.

Once the young leave their mother, they may travel in a group for a few days. Then they separate.

This mountain lion cub is six weeks old.

Each begins searching for a home range of its own. They may roam quite a distance, across the home ranges of many adult lions. Mountain lions are able to breed by the time they are three years old. However, they will not do so if they have not found a home range.

In captivity, mountain lions have lived to be twenty years old. Those living free in the wild usually die younger.

CHAPTER FOUR:

Jaguar, ocelot, jaguarundi, margay

There are a few other wild cats in North America, too. They are the jaguar, ocelot, jaguarundi, and margay cat.

These cats live throughout Mexico and South America. At one time, they also lived throughout the southwestern United States — as far east as Louisiana and as far north as Colorado. As land in the Southwest was settled and developed, however, they were pushed to the south. Today, they exist in the United States mainly as wanderers across the border from Mexico. Only a few still live in the southwestern United States.

The jaguar looks much like a spotted mountain lion. It has the same general build, but it is bigger and heavier. It often weighs more than two hundred pounds (90 kg). Its lips are black. This makes its teeth look very fierce! Scientists call the jaguar *Felis onca.* People in Central and South America call it "el tigre," or "the tiger."

The ocelot is a small, spotted cat with a long tail. It

may measure two-and-a-half to four feet (0.8-1.2m) in total length, including its tail. It is yellowish-brown, with dark brown stripes and spots on its back. The ocelot also has two black stripes on its cheeks and black rings on its tail. Its fur is sleek and glossy. It is often called the most beautiful cat in the world. In Central and South America, it is known as "el tigrillo," or "the little tiger." Scientists have named it *Felis pardalis.*

The jaguarundi is a plain-colored small cat, with no spots or stripes at all. It has a long, slender body with a small head, short legs, and a long tail. It looks a bit like a weasel. The jaguarundi may be no bigger than a large house cat. Some jaguarundi are gray and some are red. Litters may have both colors. All have lighter underparts. The jaguarundi may live in small

Many people think that the ocelot is the most beautiful wild cat.

groups, even as adults. Scientists have named it *Felis yajouaroundi.*

The margay cat is a small cat, like the jaguarundi, but it is spotted. It looks like a small ocelot with a long tail. Scientists call it *Felis wiedii.*

All these lesser-known cats have much the same mating habits as the lynx, bobcat, and mountain lion. The exception is the jaguar. Although the job is done mainly by the mother, both parents help raise the jaguar cubs. The jaguar may breed at any time of the year, just like the mountain lion.

These four southern cats like brushy areas with lots of cover. This is one of the reasons so few of them live in the United States today. Most of their natural, brushy habitat has been destroyed.

A jaguarundi stalks its prey.

CHAPTER FIVE:

Once they become adults, the wild cats of North America are not often pursued as prey by larger predators. Bears and coyotes may kill a few. And once in a while, a mountain lion may prey upon a lynx or bobcat. The wild cats' worst enemy is mankind. Humans kill wild cats as pests, if the cats have attacked their livestock. They also hunt them for sport and sometimes food. In addition, the lynx and bobcat are regularly trapped so that their pelts can be sold on the fur-trading market. The habitat that these cats need to survive is sometimes destroyed to make way for housing developments and resort areas in the mountains.

But the lynx, bobcat, and mountain lion are all doing quite well in North America today — except for the small population of mountain lions living in Florida. There are so few mountain lions left there that they could become extinct, just like they have in other parts of their original range.

This Florida mountain lion, which people often call the Florida panther, is listed as an endangered species by the United States government. Its life is now protected. It can no longer be killed. If people respect the law and help preserve its habitat, the mountain lion may be saved in Florida.

MAP:

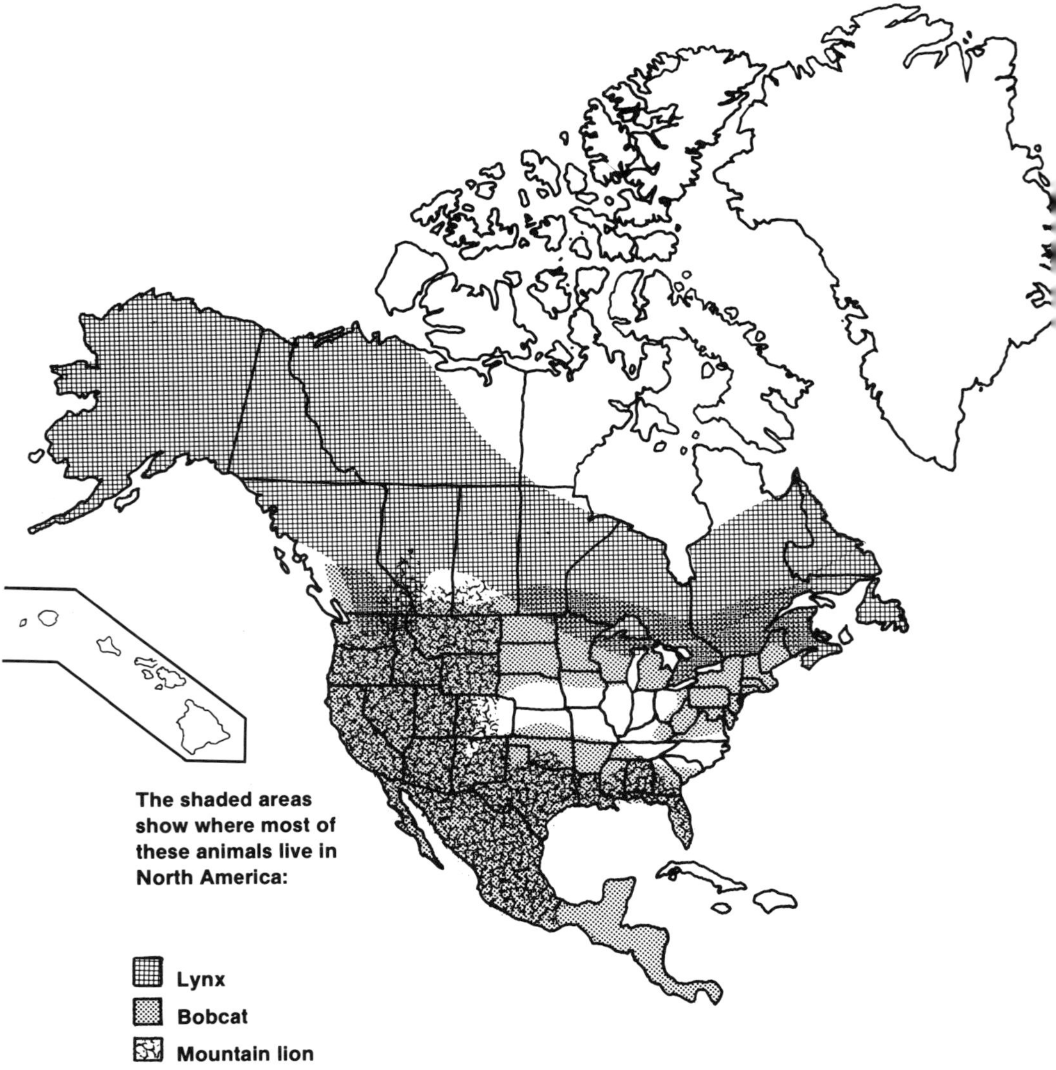

The shaded areas show where most of these animals live in North America:

INDEX/GLOSSARY:

ALTRICIAL 12 — *Not fully developed when born; altricial animals are not able to leave the place of their birth for quite awhile and must be cared for.*
ARMADILLO 36 — *A toothless, burrowing mammal with bony plates that look like armor*
BOUNTY 29 — *A reward, usually money, paid to individuals for killing certain animals.*
BUFF 27 — *A pail yellow color.*
CACHE 21
CAMOUFLAGE 40
CARCASS 22, 39 — *The dead body of any animal.*
CARNIVORES 7 — *A flesh-eating mammal.*
CREVICE: 9 —*A narrow opening in a rock, usually caused by a crack that has split.*
CUBS 12, 27, 40
DECIDUOUS 34 — *Walking on the toes, rather than on the soles of the feet, with the heels not touching the ground.*
DEN 20, 40
DIET 7, 21, 30, 36
DIGITIGRADE 11 — *A tree that sheds its leave annually.*
DORMANT 9 — *The time when an animal loses part of its power of sensation and goes to sleep; a time of inactivity.*
ENEMY 45
EXTINCT 29, 45
EYES 9
GESTATION PERIOD 27, 40
HABITAT 15, 30, 34 — *The environment in which an animal usually lives.*
HIBERNATE 9 — *That time during the winter when an animal loses all of its powers of sensation and goes to sleep.*
HOME RANGE 19, 34
HUNTING BEDS 22
LIFESPAN 28, 41
MAMMALS 21 — *The animals whose females nurse their young.*
MATING 26, 40
MOLT 18, 34 — *To shed the hair at certain times of the year.*
MUSKEY BOG 15 — *A marsh formed by the deposit of thick layers of decaying vegetable matter.*
NOCTURNAL 10, 19 — *Active at night.*
PAPILLAE 9
PERSONALITIES 12
PHYSICAL CHARACTERISTICS 16, 29, 42
PREDATORS 7 — *An animal that hunts and kills another animal for food.*
PREY 21 — *An animal that is hunted and killed by another animal as food.*
PUPIL 10 — *The opening at the center of the eye.*
RANGE 6, 14, 29, 42
RETRACTILE 11 — *Something that can be drawn back or in.*
SIZE 17, 33, 42
SOUNDS 5, 26, 36
STRANGULATION 22 — *Killed by having the throat squeezed so that the air supply to the lungs is cut off.*

WILDLIFE
HABITS & HABITAT

READ AND ENJOY THE SERIES:

THE WHITETAIL • THE PHEASANT

THE BALD EAGLE • THE WOLVES

THE SQUIRRELS • THE BEAVER

THE GRIZZLY • THE MALLARD

THE RACCOON • THE WILD CATS

THE RATTLESNAKE • THE SHEEP

THE ALLIGATOR • THE CARIBOU

THE CANADA GOOSE • THE FOXES